I0021582

QUICK STEPS
A QUICKSTEP INTO COMPUTER PROGRAMMING
& PROBLEM-SOLVING

2018 EDITION

Lenghorne

© 2018

By. A.D. Vanhorne

QUICK STEPS

A QUICKSTEP INTO COMPUTER PROGRAMMING
& PROBLEM SOLVING

SECOND EDITION

Adrian D. VANHORNE
Department of Computer Studies
The Mico University College
1 A Marescaux Road
Kingston 5
Jamaica

First Edition
First Printing – 2008
Reprinted 2018

© **A.D Vanhorne**

 © 2018 by Lenghorne, Patrick Drive, Grange Hill
P.O, Westmoreland, Jamaica.

The author and publisher of this book have used their best efforts in preparing this book. These efforts include the development, research, and testing of the theories and programs to determine their effectiveness. The concepts used in this book have been simplified to meet the needs of the beginner programmer. Therefore no prior Programming experience is required to use this book.

Printed in Jamaica

© **2018 by A.D. Vanhorne**

ISBN-13: 978-1986545938
ISBN-10: 1986545938

Contents

Introduction

INTRODUCTION

Programs add meaning to a computer. A simple desktop computer can be converted into a flight simulator, entertainment center or just a resource center. This transformation is dependent on the programs that are added to the computer.

There are two main types of programs: System programs and Application programs. The system programs control the operations that go on among the various hardware that make up the computer while the application program is designed to solve specific problems.

It is therefore very important that we learn how to write programs since it creates a new approach towards the use of the computer.

In this text, we will focus on the steps involved in writing programs. The text is intended for beginner programmers. Therefore you do not require prior experience of programming to use this text. It is truly a Quick Step into Computer Programming and Problem Solving.

UNIT I

The Computer

A computer is a machine that accepts an INPUT and PROCESSES the input to produce an OUTPUT. Some computers are also capable of storing or holding data for future use.

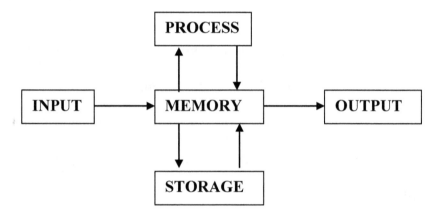

The computer cannot work without instruction in its memory.

Program

A program is a set of coded instructions that may be added to the computer's memory to tell it what to do and how to perform different tasks. Programs are normally written in programming languages such as Java, Pascal, FORTRAN, C++, C, Visual Basic and so on.

There are two main levels of programming languages: High level and Low-Level. The lower the level of the programming language is the easier it is for the computer to understand it.

How are programs written?

Information that is given to us is normally written in a language, such as English or Spanish. However, most of us understand only English; therefore if another language is communicated to us, it must be converted to English in order for us to understand and use it.

Programs are also written in languages known as programming languages. Like us, the language that the computer understands is **Machine language (1s and 0s)**, therefore if programs are written in other languages; they must be converted back to machine language for the computer to understand and use them.

Programming languages are classified into five major categories: first generation (Machine Language), second generation (Assembly languages), third generation languages, fourth generation languages and fifth generation (natural languages). **Machine** and **Assembly** languages are referred to as low-level languages; third generation, fourth generation, and natural languages are called high-level languages.

A **low-level language** is written to run on a particular computer. A **high-level language** can run on many different computers.

Low-Level Languages

Machine language (First-generation) **-** this is the native language of the computer system. It is the only language that the computer understands directly. Machine language instructions use a series of (1s and 0s) that correspond to the on and off state of a computer.

11110101	110001011
10001010	101010101
11010101	101010111

Advantage

1.   It makes fast and efficient use of the CPU (codes execute fast since no translation is needed).

Disadvantage

1.   Codes are machine dependent (they are not portable to other computers)

2.   Coding in 1s and 0s of machine language can be tedious and time-consuming

The challenges in writing machine language instructions led to the development of the second generation of programming language (assembly languages).

3

Assembly Languages (second generation) – this is a symbolic form of machine language. With assembly language, instructions are written using abbreviations and codes known as mnemonics, which are easier to understand than machine language.

```
LIM 0   LAD A
ADD C  SAD T
```

Advantages

1. Symbolic instruction codes (mnemonics) are easier to understand than strings of 1s and 0s.
2. Programmers can refer to storage locations using symbolic addresses (instead of using the actual numeric location, symbols can be used)
3. It is considered more secure since fewer persons understand it

Disadvantages

1. Programs are machine specific
2. Codes must be translated into machine language before the computer can understand them.
3. It is difficult to learn

*The program that is used to convert the assembly language to machine language is known as an **assembler**.*

High-Level Languages

The disadvantage of low-level languages (machine and assembly) led to the development of high-level languages in the late 1950s and 1960s.

Third generation language (3GL) instruction is written as a series of English like words. For example 'PRINT' to display information on the screen, 'Read' to get an Input and so on. Third generation language is also known as procedural languages. Examples of 3GL are Pascal, C, and Quick Basic. As in an assembly language program, the 3GL code is called source code (program) and it must be converted to machine language for the computer to understand it. For third generation languages, the translation is performed using one of two types of programs: Compiler or an interpreter.

PASCAL	C	QBASIC

Program HelloWorld;
 	
Uses Crt;
Begin
  Write('Hello World');
End.
	# include<conio.h>
	
	void main()
	{
	  printf("Hello World");
	}
		PRINT "Hello World"

Program Translators

Programs that are not written in machine language have to be translated to machine language before the computer can use them. The two main translators that are used to convert high-

level languages to machine language are Compiler and
Interpreter.

Compiler

A **compiler** converts the entire source code to machine
language codes, at one time. The machine language code that is
generated by the compiler is known as an **object code**. The
object code/program can be executed repeatedly.

The relationship between source code, compiler and object
code

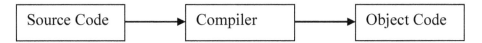

| Source Code | Compiler | Object Code |

Advantage of Compiling

1.   Compiling is faster than interpreting since the entire
       program is converted at once
2.   Once an object code is generated, it can be used
       repeatedly without recompilation

Disadvantage of Compiling

1.   Errors are not detected until the entire program is
       compiled

Interpreter

While a compiler translates an entire program code at once, an interpreter translates one program statement (line) at a time. That is it reads and converts one line to machine language before moving on to the next.

Advantage

1.   It immediately displays feedback when it finds a syntax error (the programmer can correct any error before evaluation of the next line)

Disadvantage

1.   Interpreted programs do not run as fast as compiled programs because the program must be translated to machine language each time it is executed.

Some programming languages contain both compiler and interpreter. The interpreter is normally used for debugging and then the compiler is used when the program is ready to be delivered to the user.

Fourth Generation Languages (4GL) – this is a nonprocedural language, which means the programmer only specifies what the program should accomplish, without explaining how. Coding in 4GL requires much less time and effort of the programmer.

4GL language is very easy to use and learn. Most 4GLs are associated with a database and its project dictionary. Example of 4GL is the standard query language (SQL) found in most database management systems.

Natural Languages – sometimes called fifth generation language, is a type of query language that allows the user to enter requests that resemble speech. For example, an SQL query to obtain a list of students name would be **SELECT FIRSTNAME, LASTNAME FROM STUDENT**. However, in natural language, the query might be **<u>TELL ME THE NAMES OF THE STUDENTS.</u>** Natural language is often associated with expert systems and artificial intelligence.

UNIT II

Problem Partitioning

A programming task often has the following sub-processes:

- INPUT- Getting something from the user
- PROCESS- an action to change data into information
- OUTPUT- Getting a result from the computer
- STORAGE- Putting away information for later use

Study the following scenario and try to identify the input, output, processing and storage operations:

(i)   Computing the cost of a 3GHz Dual Core CPU after 25% discount

(ii)   Dialing the number for your technician to get the speed and type of CPU to buy

(iii)   Reading the report about the CPU failure from your technician

(iv)   Saving money to buy the CPU

(v)   Asking your salesperson the cost and discount on his Dual-Core CPUs

(b)   Place the tasks labeled (i) to (v) in Part (a) above in the CORRECT sequence.

* Share your answer with your friends and see how you both did.

* Check the Answer Sheet for another possible Solution.

If the answer to (b) above is correct, then you would have successfully written an algorithm to replace a broken CPU. *An algorithm is a sequence of step-by-step procedures that may be followed to successfully solve a problem.*

This is what I do to prepare the Johnnycake dough for mom:

1.   Get ½ of flour

2.   Get ¼ tsp of baking powder

3.   Get ¼ tsp of salt

4.   I get an empty bowl

5.   Mix the flour, baking powder, and salt in the bowl
6.   Get a ¼ cup of water
7.   Pour the water into the bowl and mix it until a doe is formed, then mamma fries the doe in small portions.

What should I do in order to make myself a cup of lemon aid?

Algorithms are written using a set of English like statements know as *Pseudocode*, or they may be represented graphically in *flow charts*. In writing pseudocodes, the following verbs may be used interchangeably to define a problem:

INPUT	PROCESS	OUTPUT	STORAGE
INPUT	SET	PRINT	WRITE
READ	LET	DISPLAY	ASSIGN
GET		WRITE	

Interpreting a Programming question
This is the recommended approach for writing your programs:
1.   Try to get a good understanding of the problem. (definition).

2.   Identify possible methods of solving the problem.

3.   Select one of those methods to solve the problem.

4.   Test the solution; i.e. check if the problem was solved

5.   If the problem was solved stop here, otherwise repeat step three (select another possible solution).

Whenever you see a programming question, bear in mind the four functions outlined in the table above (input, output, processing, storage). Read each line and either circle or underline verbs that are related to any of the functions listed.

Example: <u>Get</u> a number from the user <u>find</u> its square and <u>print</u>
the square.

The underlined verbs (actions):

- Get ☺
- Find
- Print

*Now try to match these three verbs to the functions outlined
above. Remember that the action will be performed by a
computer. So let us think 'like a computer'*

*1ˢᵗ verb – Get: How does the computer get data? Remember
that devices like the keyboard, mouse etc are used to enter data
into the computer. Therefore Get in this case is suggesting an
INPUT action.*

*2ⁿᵈ verb – Find: The very nature of this word indicates a set of
actions to be performed in order to get the square. We are also
reminded that the computer should find the square of the
number entered. In other words, the computer will be working
on the number to get its square. (Whenever the computer
manipulate data to get information, like in this case it is
<u>processing</u>)*

*3ʳᵈ verb – Print: Whenever the computer prints or displays a
result, it is simply sending out information to the user.
Therefore this would be an Output.*

We could then refine our problem as follows:

INPUT a number
Compute its square (square * Square)
Print the square

The following pages will look at each action in more detail and
with some easy to follow examples.

In order to be successful, you must commit yourself to doing all the activities in this text. Program with FUN!

INPUT

Example 1
Write an algorithm to read a number from the user.

Think with me now as if you are the computer. :)

READ suggests getting something from outside. For the computer to read a number, the user must enter one. However, when we are writing pseudocodes, we use variables to represent the numbers.

1. A variable is a name that is used to represent a value and this value is capable of changing. Example: X, Y, Karen, Sum and so on.

2. Let's use the **Variable 'X'** to represent the number that the user will enter.

Solution

Algorithm	Pseudocode
Get a number	**INPUT X**

*The pseudocode is a more structured form of the algorithm.

Example 2
Write an algorithm to read TWO numbers from the user.

In this case we are still reading, however at this point we need two numbers; therefore we will use two variables

Lets use X and Y (You could use any two variables)

SOLUTION

INPUT X, Y

13

Activity 1

Write an algorithm that accepts a student's Address, Telephone number, and Identification number.

HINT
There are three variables, try to identify them first!

Activity 2

Mr. James would like to calculate the volume of water that his rectangular swimming pool can hold. He has hired you to create an algorithm that will allow his Gardener to enter the length, width, and height of the pool, in order to perform the calculation.

Discuss your answers with your teacher and your friends.

Example 1

Write an algorithm to display the line "Hello Jamaica" on the screen.

Display, in this case, suggests, putting out something on a screen for the user to read. Therefore since we are sending out something, it MUST be an OUTPUT. To display a text on the screen we write it in quotations ("Hello Jamaica"), however, if we were displaying a variable we just use the variable name (e.g X)

SOLUTION

PRINT "Hello Jamaica"

Example 2

Given that Answer=X+Y, Print a text saying "The answer is:" followed by the answer.

In this case we will be printing a text, followed by a variable in the form – Answer
As indicated earlier, the text will be written in quotations, but the variable will remain as it is

SOLUTION

PRINT "The answer is:"
PRINT Answer

Think with me now as if you are the computer. :)

15

ASSIGNMENT STATEMENT

An assignment statement is used to put a value in a variable and for defining constants. In our mathematics class, the assignment statement that we are most accustomed to is equal "=".

For this text, we will be using the equal sign for comparison operations and the arrow "←" as our assignment statement. The ← is independent of all Programming Languages.

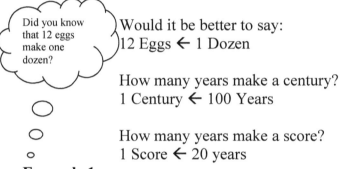

Did you know that 12 eggs make one dozen?

Would it be better to say:
12 Eggs ← 1 Dozen

How many years make a century?
1 Century ← 100 Years

How many years make a score?
1 Score ← 20 years

Example 1

Three boys decide to save some money on a weekly basis; there is no fixed amount that is saved by each boy:

One week, they decided to save as follows:
- Roy = 200
- Bob = 150
- Kenny = 400

Study the pattern above and write one line that indicates how the total saving may be calculated. Bear in mind that the savings may vary on a weekly basis.

Each boy's amount is store/ assign to his name. Since the savings may change on a weekly basis, it would not be wise to tell the computer to add 200, 150 and 400 each week.

It would be more flexible to tell the computer to add the amount stored in each boy's name on a weekly basis. Therefore:

Sum ← Roy + Bob + Kenny

Example 2

A bartender accidentally pours Beer in a soup bowl (container A), and Soup in a Beer Mug (container B). Explain with aid of assignment statements how the bartender may correct his mistake.

➢ She cannot mix the soup and the beer together
➢ Both containers are full. What do you think?
➢ I think she needs a third container (C)

STEP 1: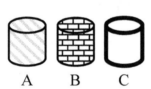

        A   B   C

STEP 2:   Put the content of container A INTO container **C**

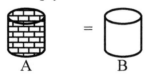

        C   A
        C = A {Container A is now empty}

STEP 3:   Put the content of container B into A, since A is empty:

        A   B

STEP 4:   Container B is now empty, so we can pour
                 the content of container C into container B:

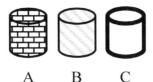

B   C

MISSION ACCOMPLISH, THE Containers
NOW HAVE THE CORRECT SUBSTANCES

A   B   C

Container C no longer store anything.

Just to sum up the swapping that took place:

C ← A
A ← B
B ← C

*That's what we did folks.

Flow Chart

An algorithm can be expressed diagrammatically in a flow
chart. The basic symbols in a flowchart are:

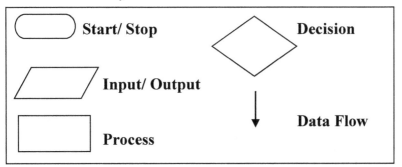

USING INPUT AND ASSIGNMENT STATEMENTS

In this section, we will be using INPUT and assignment statements to solve basis Mathematical Problems. You will be presented with a problem and its solution, after which you will get practice activities:

An algorithm is required to get two numbers from the user, in the variables: A and B. Calculate and store the total of A and B in a variable name Sum.

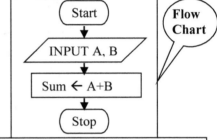

SOLUTION

INPUT A, B
Sum ← A + B

Activity 1

Write an algorithm to get a number from the user in the variable num, and calculate the Square of num and store it in the variable Sq.

SOLUTION

INPUT num
Sq ← num * num

Activity 2

Write an algorithm to get two numbers from the user in the variables: **Joy**, and **Peace**. Compute the Product of Joy and Peace and store the Result in **Love**.

* Compare your answer with the answer your friends got, then show your teacher.

Activity 3

Write an algorithm do the following:
1. Get three numbers from the user, in three variables of your choice
2. Calculate the sum of the numbers and store it in a variable of your choice
3. Calculate the average of the three numbers and store it in a variable of your choice

Activity 4

Study the following algorithm and explain what it does:

GCT_Rate ← 0.165
INPUT Price
GCT ← Price * GCT_Rate
Total ← Price + GCT

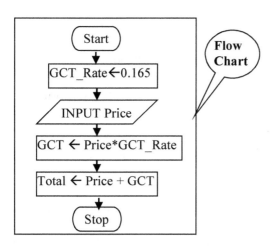

INPUT, OUTPUT AND ASSIGNMENT STATEMENTS

In this section, we will be focusing on how we can use our Input, Output and Assignment statements to solve problems.

An algorithm is required to get two numbers from the user, in the variables: A and B. Calculate and store the total of A and B in a variable name Sum. Print the sum of the two numbers.

SOLUTION

```
INPUT A, B
Sum ← A + B
PRINT Sum
```

Activity 1

Write an algorithm to:
1. Print a text to tell the user to enter a number
2. Get a number from the user in the variable num,
3. Calculate the Square of num and store it in the variable Sq.
4. Print the Value of Sq

SOLUTION

```
PRINT "Please enter a number"
INPUT num
    Sq ← num * num
    PRINT Sq
```

Activity 2

Write an algorithm to get two numbers from the user in the variables: **Joy**, and **Peace (Before you get Joy or Peace,** Write a statement to prompt the user to enter the value for Joy/ Peace). Compute the Product of Joy and Peace and store the Result in **Love**. Print the value of Love on the screen

* Compare your answer with the answer your friends got, then show your teacher.

Activity 3

Write an algorithm do the following:
1. PRINT a statement on the screen to ask for each number
2. Get three numbers from the user, in three variables of your choice
3. Calculate the sum of the numbers and store it in a variable of your choice
4. Calculate the average of the three numbers and store it in a variable of your choice
5. Print the result of Average

Activity 4

Study the following algorithm and explain what it does:

```
GCT_Rate ← 0.165
PRINT "Please enter the Price"
INPUT Price
GCT ← Price * GCT_Rate
Total ← Price + GCT
PRINT GCT
PRINT "The total cost is", Total
```

UNIT III

CONDITIONAL STATEMENTS

The two control structures that we will focus on in this unit are Sequence and Selection.

Sequence Control Structure

The algorithms that we have written so far use the sequence control structure. If you take a close notice, you would see that the lines of the codes are executed in a linear order i.e. line 1, then line 2 and so on. However, sometimes the programmer may want line 1 to be executed followed by line 3; to achieve this task, the selection control structure has to be used, to make the decision.

Selection (IF..THEN... ENDIF)

The selection control structure (Conditional statements) allows you to make decisions in a program.

IF (Condition is true) THEN Statement...... Statement...... Statement...... ENDIF	IF (Condiotion is true)THEN Statement...... Statement...... ELSE Statement...... Statement...... ENDIF

Basic Comparison Operators

Name	Operator
Equality	=
Greater than...............................	>
Lesser than	<
Greater than or equal.....................	>=
Lesser than or equal	<=
Not Equal	<>
Modulation.................................	Mod

Example 1

Write an algorithm to read two numbers from the user, calculate the sum, and product. Print the Sum and the Product of the two numbers, if the first number is larger than the second.

SOLUTION
INPUT X, Y
Sum ← X + Y
Product ← X * Y
IF X > Y THEN
        PRINT Sum, Product
ENDIF

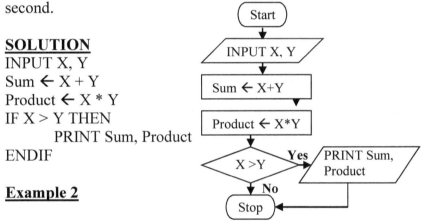

Example 2

The Sports committee has decided to regulate the admission to the annual Sports Day as follows:

Grades	Fees
7	$50
8	$60
9	$70
10	$80
11	90
Adults	100

Given that students are admitted by groups; write an algorithm to get the grade and the number of students in a group, and calculate and print the corresponding fee to be charged.

SOLUTION

```
INPUT group, amount
IF(group = 7)THEN
        Fee ← amount * 50
ENDIF
IF(group = 8)THEN
        Fee ← amount * 60
ENDIF
IF(group = 9)THEN
        Fee ← amount * 70
ENDIF
IF(group = 10)THEN
        Fee ← amount * 80
ENDIF
IF(group = 11)THEN
        Fee ← amount * 90
ENDIF
IF(group = "adult")THEN
        Fee ← amount * 100
ENDIF
PRINT Fee
```

Task 1

The 4-H club decides to charge a late fee of $10 per minute for members who arrive at the meeting after 5:00 pm. Write a pseudocode to get the number of minutes a member is late, and calculate and print the late fee to be charged.

Example 3

Write an algorithm/pseudocode to read a number from the user; multiply it by -5 and store the result in P if the number is negative. IF the number is positive, add 20 to it and store the result in K

SOLUTION

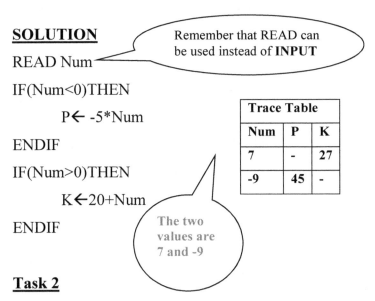

READ Num

IF(Num<0)THEN

    P← -5*Num

ENDIF

IF(Num>0)THEN

    K←20+Num

ENDIF

Remember that READ can be used instead of **INPUT**

Trace Table		
Num	P	K
7	-	27
-9	45	-

The two values are 7 and -9

Task 2

Write a pseudocode to get a number from the user. If the number entered is negative, calculate the square of the number. However, if the number is positive, compute the cube of the number. Print the result of square and cube.

IF THEN ....ELSE

Most times we carry out an action there is often an alternate action. E.g. But a patty and a Fruit Punch Box Drink for me; IF there is no Fruit Punch, buy a Pine Apple Drink.

The keyword 'ELSE', is often used with the IF statement to direct the computer to an alternative action to carry out. ELSE is mainly used where one of two possible answers is correct (Boolean).

Example 4

Write an algorithm to read a student's gender and print the registration room, based on the following:

Girls   -   Room9

Boys   -   Room1

SOLUTION

INPUT gender

IF gender = "male" THEN

      PRINT "Register at Room1"

ELSE

      PRINT "Register at Room9"

ENDIF

Example 5

Consider the following

INPUT X, Y, Z

Y ← X + Y
X ← X – Y
Y ← X + Y
IF X > Y THEN
     Z ← X – Y – Z
ELSE
     Z ← X + Y + Z
ENDIF
PRINT X, Y, Z

WHAT IS PRINTED BY THE
ALGORITHM IF THE INPUT IS:
a. 1,1,1   b. 1, 2, 3

SOLUTION

Trace Table					
x	y	z	x	y	z
1	1	1	1	2	3
1	2	1	1	3	3
-1	2	1	-2	3	3
-1	1	1	-2	1	3
-1	1	1	-2	1	2
Print -1, 1,1			Print -2, 1, 2		

28

Repetition in a program is achieved through the use of loops. In this unit, we will focus on the following repetition structures

1. WHILE	2. REPEAT
3. FOR	4. DO…WHILE

The **WHILE** Repetition Structure

This repetition structure allows the programmer to specify that an action is to be repeated while some conditions remain true. Example:

> While there are more items on my shopping list
>> Purchase next item and cross it off my list

Example 1
Write an algorithm to read the names of a set of students until a student by the name: "Herfa" is entered.

1	INPUT name	Get the first student's name
2	WHILE name <> "Herfa" DO	Check if the name is not Herfa
3	INPUT name	Since the name is not Herfa cont to line 3 and get a name. cont Line 2.
4	ENDWHILE	End of Loop

Example 2
Consider a program segment designed to find the first power of 2 larger than 1000. Suppose the integer value **product** has been initialized to 2. When the following WHILE repetition structure finishes executing, the **product** will contain the desired answer:

Product ← 2
WHILE(product <=1000)
        Product ← 2 * Product
ENDWHILE

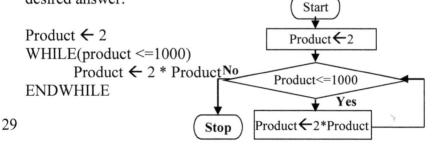

29

Example 3

The following data represents some sample score obtained by students in a test:

5,   4,   7,   10,   0,   6,   1,   0,   9,
    8,   999

999 is the dummy value which terminates the data. Write a pseudocode to read any data in the above format, and print the number of students scoring 0 and the number scoring 10

1	Zcount ← 0
2	Tcount ← 0
3	INPUT num
4	WHILE (num <> 999) DO
5	IF (num = 0) THEN
6	Zcount ← Zcount + 1
7	ENDIF
8	IF(num = 10)THEN
9	Tcount ← Tcount + 1
10	ENDIF
11	INPUT num
12	END WHILE
13	PRINT Zcount, Tcount

What is this saying?
In lines 1 and 2, Zcount and Tcount are set to zero, in order to facilitate the counting from one. At line 3 we get the first number from the user. At the WHILE statement, we check if the number entered is 999 (if it was 999, we would stop there); however if it is not 999, it would continue to line 5. IF num is 0, Zcount is incremented (increased by 1), and if num is 10 Tcount is incremented.
At line 11 we get a new number and continue the loop until num is 999
When the loop ends, we move to line 13, where the value of Zcount and Tcount are printed.

EXAMPLE 4

Write a pseudocode to read in THREE numbers and print the highest and lowest number.

SOLUTION

```
count ← 0
WHILE count <=3 DO
        count ← count + 1

        INPUT num
        IF count = 1 THEN
                SMALLEST ← num
                LARGEST ← num
        ENDIF
        IF num > LARGEST THEN
                LARGEST ← num
        ENDIF
        IF num < SMALLEST THEN
                SMALLEST ← NUM
        ENDIF
ENDWHILE
```

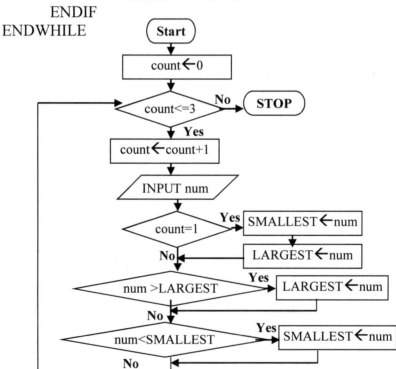

31

Activity 1

Write a pseudocode to simulate the order process at your local KFC as described below:

a.   Get the name, quantity, and price of a set of items from the user

b.   Calculate the Total cost

c.   Repeat the procedures above until an item by the name "end" is entered.

d.   Print the Final cost at the end

Activity 2

Write a pseudocode to assist the teachers at your school in registering students for the school year. It is not sure how many students will be attending registration.

a.   Get the name and class of each student

b.   Calculate the amount of student registering for 7a, and 7b

c.   Keep getting students' information until the name "Freda" is entered

d.   At the end of the pseudocode print the number of students registered for 7a and 7b

The **FOR** Repetition Structure

The FOR loop repeats a port of a program a fixed number of times. The repetition is usually controlled by a counter. E.g. running four hundred meters on a two hundred meter track; in this race, the athlete would run two times around the track.

Example 1:
Consider an algorithm for running a four hundred meter on a two hundred meter track.

    FOR count = 1 to 2 DO
            Run around the track
    ENDFOR

Example 2

Write a pseudocode to read ten numbers from the user.

Method 1 {Using 10 different variables}

SOLUTION
INPUT A
INPUT B
INPUT C
INPUT D
INPUT E
INPUT F
INPUT G
INPUT H
INPUT I
INPUT J

* Note the letters A to J represents the ten different variables

Method 2 {Using the FOR loop}

SOLUTION
FOR COUNT = 1 TO 10 DO
INPUT NUM
ENDFOR

* The statement "INPUT NUM" will be repeated ten times (because of the loop).

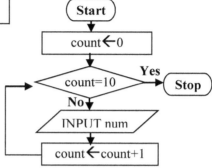

EXAMPLE 3

Write a pseudocode to read in THREE numbers and print the highest and lowest number.

SOLUTION
FOR count = 1 to 3 DO
INPUT num
IF count = 1 THEN
SMALLEST ← num
LARGEST ← num
ENDIF
IF num > LARGEST THEN
LARGEST ← num
ENDIF
IF num < SMALLEST THEN
SMALLEST ← NUM
ENDIF
ENDFOR

What is this saying?
We need three numbers; therefore the count is from 1 to 3. The first number entered by the user will automatically be the smallest and largest at the moment. The other numbers are compared against the first. Therefore if the second number is a greater than the largest (the first number); then the Largest will now be the second number, so Largest=num, likewise if the number is less than the smallest number. Smallest= num

34

Activity 1

Football Depot decides to sponsor the shoe for each member of your school's football team.
Write a pseudocode to get the size shoe of each member of your school football team.

Activity 2

Write a program to read ten numbers from the user, and calculate and print their sum and average.

Activity 3

Write a pseudocode to do the following:
a.   Read the number of students in a class.
b.   For each student, get his/ her name, and gender

Activity 4

Write a pseudocode to do the following:
a.   Read the number of students in a class.
b.   For each student, get his/ her name, and gender
c.   Calculate and print the amount of male and the number of female students in the class

UNIT V

A trace table is a technique used to test algorithms, in order to make sure that no logical errors occur whilst the algorithm is being processed. The table usually takes the form of a multi-column, multi-row table; with each column showing a variable, and each row showing each number inputted into the algorithm and the subsequent values of the variables.

Trace tables are typically used in schools and colleges when teaching students how to program, they can be an essential tool in teaching students how a certain algorithm works and the systematic process that is occurring when the algorithm is executed.

They can also be useful for debugging applications, using a trace table can help a programmer easily detect what error is occurring, and why it may be occurring.

Example
$x \leftarrow 0$
For i = 1 to 5
   $x \leftarrow x+i$
End for

i	x
1	1
2	3
3	6
4	10
5	15

This example shows the systematic process that takes place whilst the algorithm is processed, as the values of I and x change, their new values are recorded in the trace table, this example shows why trace tables are useful for debugging and in education, they make following an algorithmic process easy to follow and understand.

Example 2

Using a trace table, determine what is printed by the following algorithm:

LINE	CODE
1	A ← 3
2	B ← 5
3	Sum ← 1
4	WHILE B <= 10
5	B ← B + A
6	Sum ← Sum + B
7	END WHILE

Trace Table

A	B	SUM
3	5	1
3	8	9
3	11	20

In lines 1 to 3 the variables A, B, and Sum are initialized to 3, 5, and 1 respectively. In the trace table, the variable names form the heading, and we enter the values of the variables (see line 1 of the trace table) below the respective headings.

*Line **4** of the algorithm has (WHILE B <= 10), if it is true that B is lesser than or equal to 10, then the program will proceed to line 5, otherwise it would stop at line 4 and jump to line 7 to terminate. However, in this case, the value of B is 5 and 5 is lesser than 10 so it would go to line 5.*

In line 5, the value of B changes to (5+3=8), therefore we move to the second line of the trace table to write the 8 for B. Sum also changes to (1+8=9). Since we are in a loop, the algorithm will move back to line 4 to check if the condition is still true. The value of B which is 8, is lesser than 10, so it would once again move to line 5. At line 5 the value of B changes to (8 + 3 = 11), 11 is now written in the third line of the trace table. The sum will also change to (9 + 11 = 20), this 20 will be written in the third line of the trace table.

The algorithm then moves to line 4, to check if the condition is still true. However B is now 11 and 11 is not lesser than or equal to 10, therefore it will jump to line 7 and terminate.

The value of A did not change throughout it is rewritten as 3.

Example 3
State the output of the following algorithm, if MARK is 50:

(i)   READ MARK
        IF mark < 40THEN
             PRINT 'The student has failed'
        Else
             PRINT 'Let us see'

MARK	PRINT
50	Let us see

This is printed since Mark = 50 and 50 is not lesser then 40.

(ii)   WHILE (mark <> 50) DO
        BEGIN
             MARK ← MARK + 2
             PRINT 'Working'
        ENDWHILE
        PRINT 'The student has passed'

This is printed since the WHILE condition is false. Mark is 50. If mark was not 50 it would print 'Working'

MARK	PRINT
50	The student has passed

Example 4

Copy and complete the following trace table for the following algorithm, given that the number 4 is the input value for X.

READ X
FOR M = 1 to X DO
$$Y \leftarrow X - M$$
$$Z \leftarrow 5 * Y - M$$
ENDFOR
PRINT Z

Trace Table

X	M	Y	Z
4	1	3	14
4	2	2	8
4	3	1	2
4	4	0	-4

PRINT_____-4_____

In this case, the last value you get for Z will be printed, since the Print statement is outside the loop.

Multiplication is normally done before addition and subtraction.

Task 1

Create a trace table for the following algorithm, given that the INPUT values for num are: 100, 30, 200

```
FOR count = 1 to 3 DO
        INPUT num
        IF count = 1 THEN
                SMALLEST ← num
                LARGEST ← num
        ENDIF
        IF num > LARGEST THEN
                LARGEST ← num
        ENDIF
        IF num < SMALLEST THEN
                SMALLEST ← NUM
        ENDIF
ENDFOR
```

Task 2

Create a Trace Table for the following algorithm:

```
Product ← 2
WHILE(Product <=10)
        Product ← 2 * Product
ENDWHILE
```

Task 3

What is printed by the following algorithm?

```
COUNT ← 1
X ← 2
WHILE COUNT < 26 DO
        X ← X + 2
        PRINT COUNT, X
        COUNT ← COUNT + 5
END WHILE
```

UNIT VI

Programming Language

In unit 1 we looked at various classes of programming languages. A programming language is an artificial language that can be used to control the behavior of a machine, particularly a computer. Programming languages are defined by syntactic and semantic rules which describe their structure and meaning respectively. Many programming languages have some form of written specification of their syntax and semantics; some are defined by an official implementation (eg, an ISO Standard), while others have a dominant implementation (eg, Perl).

Programming languages are also used to facilitate communication about the task of organizing and manipulating information, and to express algorithms precisely.

In this text, we will focus on three programming languages:
1. QUICK BASIC
2. TURBO PASCAL
3. C
We will look at how we can convert various algorithms to these languages.

Input and output statements for the different Languages

Language	Input	Output	Case Sensitive
Quick Basic	INPUT	PRINT	NO
TURBO PASCAL	READ READLN	WRITE WRITELN	NO
C	scanf	printf	YES

*When a language is case sensitive the case used to write variables and keywords are important. Example: num and NUM would be different in C since different cases are used.

Data Type

Most programming languages use various data types to describe the type of data that the different variables are can hold.

DATA TYPES	DESCRIPTION
INTEGER	Whole numbers from -32768 to 32767
CHAR	1 letter only. Any character in the ASCII character set.
STRING	up to 255 letters
FLOAT/ REAL	Floating point numbers from 1E-38 to 1E+38. (Numbers with decimal points)
BOOLEAN	Can only have the value TRUE or FALSE
WORD	The integers from 0 to 65535

For this text, we will concentrate on:
1. Integer
2. Real
3. String
4. Boolean

In our algorithms, we use the variables without defining them or indicating the type of information each variable stores. However, in languages such as Pascal and C, the programmer has to define each variable before he or she can use them in a program.

Therefore if you intend to get the base and height of a triangle; **before** writing the input statements the following definition MUST be included:

PASCAL	C
Var Base, height: real;	float Base, height;

Float/real is used for Base and height since they may be decimal values.

BASIC	PASCAL	C

INPUT Base
INPUT height
	Program Triangle;
	Uses Crt;
	Var
	   Base, height: real;
	Begin
	Read(Base);
	Read(height);
	End.
		# include<conio.h>
		float Base, height;
		void main()
		{
		scanf("%f",&Base);
		scanf("%f",&height);
		}

* No variable declaration is needed for Basic

INPUT AND OUTPUT IN PASCAL

Pascal uses two keywords to get Inputs from the user (Read and Read Line → Readln)

Read – gets an input and keep the insertion pointer in the same line

Readln – gets an input from the user and move the insertion pointer to the next line

Writeln – displays information on the user screen and move the insertion pointer to the next line

Write – displays information on the screen and keep the insertion pointer in the same line

Basic Output

Write a program to print "Hello Love" on the screen.

Quick Basic Solution is **PRINT "Hello Love"**

Pascal Solution is:
Program Greeting;
Begin
   Write('Hello World');
End.

Example:

Write an algorithm to:

1. Print a text to tell the user to enter a number
2. Get a number from the user in the variable num,
3. Calculate the Square of num and store it in the variable Sq.
4. Print the Value of Sq

Quick Basic Solution

1	PRINT "Enter a number"	An Output statement to display the message
2	INPUT num	An INPUT statement to get the value
3	Sq = num * num	The process to compute square
4	PRINT Sq	An output statement to print Square

This is similar to the pseudocode

Turbo Pascal Solution

1	Program CalSrqr;	Line 1 The program's name
2	Uses crt;	Line 2 The unit that the program uses
3	Var	Line 3: Var – variable declaration
4	Num, Sq: Integer;	Line 4: Variables and Type (Integer)
5	Begin	Line 5: Beginning of program body
6	Write('Enter a number');	Line 6: An output statement to print the text
7	Read(num);	Line 7: An INPUT statement to get num
8	Sq:=num * num;	Line 8: The process to compute square
9	Write('The square is:', Sq);	Line 9: An output statement to print Square
10	End.	Line 10: This is the End of the Program.

NOTE
Assignment statement

Pseudocode ....←

C...=

Pascal ....:=

C Solution

1	# include<conio.h>	This is a header file that supply need functions
2	int num, Sq;	Declaration of the variables that are used in the program
3		Blank space
4	void main ()	Main function header
5	{	Begin
6	printf ("Enter a number:");	An output to display the text "Enter a number" on the screen
7	scanf("%d",&num);	An input statement to get the value for num
8	Sq = num * num;	The process to compute Square
9	printf ("The square is:%d",Sq);	An output statement to display the square on the screen
10	}	End.

In the three examples above we have three different source codes. A source code is simply a program written in a programming language. In order for the machine to use the source code, it must be converted to object code, as described in **Unit 1**. An Object code is a machine language code that is produced by a compiler.

Conditional Statements

In this Section, we will look how conditional statements are implemented in Pascal and C.

Example 1: Write a program to read two numbers and a text from the user. If the text entered is 'S', calculate and print the sum of the two numbers. However, if the text entered is 'P', compute and print the product of the two numbers.

Pseudocode/ Quick Basic Solution

1.   Let's use the variables: num1 and num2 to represent the two numbers and the variable 'Text', to represent the text.

2.   <u>Solution</u>:

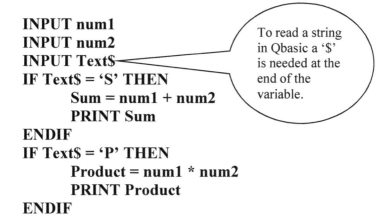

```
INPUT num1
INPUT num2
INPUT Text$
IF Text$ = 'S' THEN
        Sum = num1 + num2
        PRINT Sum
ENDIF
IF Text$ = 'P' THEN
        Product = num1 * num2
        PRINT Product
ENDIF
```

To read a string in Qbasic a '$' is needed at the end of the variable.

Turbo Pascal Solution

```
Program BigMath; {BigMath is just a name for the program}
Uses Crt;
Var
        Text: Char; {declaration of Text, to hold a single letter- Char}
        num1, num2: Integer; {num1 and num2 can only hold whole #s}
        Sum, Product: Integer; {sum and product are also integers}

Begin
        Read(num1);   {this line allows the user to enter the first number}
        Read(num2);   { this line allows the user to enter the 2nd number}
        Read(Text);   { this line allows the user to enter the 3rd number}

        IF(Text = 'S') THEN {comparison to check if the Text is 'S'}
        Begin
          Sum:=num1+num2; {this calculation will be done if Text is 'S'}
          Write(Sum); {This displays the Sum on the screen}
         End;

        IF(Text = 'P')THEN {Check if Text is 'P'}
        Begin
           Product:=num1 * num2; {calculation of product, if Text is 'P'}
           Write(Product);      {Prints the product on the user's screen}
         End;
End.
```

*the *Italicized texts explain the codes, and these are placed in curly braces referred to as comments. Anything in these curly braces will not be executed when you run the program.*

C Solution

```
# include<conio.h>

char Text;
int num1, num2, Product, Sum;

void main()
{
        scanf("%d",&num1);
        scanf("%d",&num2);
        scanf("%c",&Text);

        if(Text == 'S')
        {
                Sum = num1 + num2;
                printf("%d",Sum);
        }
        If(Text =='P')
        {
                Product = num1 * num2;
                Printf("%d",Product);
        }
}
```

The curly braces in C represent begin and end
Activity

Write a program, using the three languages described above to read a student's gender and print the registration room, based on the following:

Girls -   Room9

Boys -   Room1

REPETITION

WHILE LOOP

Example 1

Write a program to read the names of a set of students until a student by the name: "Herfa" is entered.

Quick Basic Solution

```
INPUT Studname$
WHILE Studname$ <> "Herfa"
        INPUT Studname$
WEND
```

WHILE is a pretest Loop. It performs a test for "TRUTH" before entering the loop; if that test is false then it will terminate. However if the test is true, it enters the loop, and repeat until the condition becomes false.

Turbo Pascal Solution

```
Program getherfa;

Uses crt;
Var
Studname: String;
Begin
        Read(Studname);
        WHILE (Studname <> "Herfa")DO
                Read (Studname);
End.
```

This line will be repeated until studname is "Herfa"

C Solution
```
# include <conio.h>
# include<string.h>

int Studname;

void main()
{
        scanf("%c",&Studname);
        while(strcmp(Studname, "Herfa")
                scanf("%c",&Studname);
}
```

51

Example 2

Write a program to read a set of students' name and grade, the program should terminate when a student by the name "Kamala" with grade =99 is entered. At the end of the program, print the number of students that were entered.

QUICK Basic Solution

```
Count=0
INPUT name$
INPUT grade
WHILE (name$ <> "Kamala") AND (grade <> 99) DO
        Count = Count + 1
        INPUT name$
        INPUT grade
WEND
PRINT Count
```

Count is incremented (increase by one each time in the loop).

Turbo Pascal Solution

```
Program StudCount;

Uses crt;
Var
        Name: String;
        Grade: Real;
        Count: Integer;
Begin
        Read(name);
        Read(grade);
        WHILE(name <> "Kamala") AND (grade <> 99)DO
        Begin
                Count: = Count + 1;
                Read(name);
                Read(grade);
        End;
        Write(Count);
End.
```

If these conditions are true, the lines in the loop will be executed.

{Body of the Loop}

C Solution

```c
# include<conio.h>
# include<string.h>

float grade;
char name[20];
int count;

void main()
{
        count = 0;
        scanf("%c",&name);
        scanf("%d",&grade);

        while(strcmp(name,"Kamala") && grade != 99)
        {
                count = count +1;
                scanf("%c",&name);
                scanf("%d",&grade);
        }
        printf("%d",count);
}
```

Activity

Write the following pseudocode in Quick Basic, Pascal and C:

```
X= 5
K = 5
SUM = 45

While SUM < 75 do
        SUM = SUM + K
        PRINT K
        K = K + X
EndWhile
Print SUM
```

Activity 2
Write a program to get a set of grades from the user, until the grade -1 is entered. The number of grades entered should be printed at the end of the program.

Write a program to read ten numbers from the user, and calculate and print their sum and average.

Quick Basic Solution

```
Sum = 0
FOR count = 1 to 10
        INPUT X
        Sum = Sum + x
NEXT
Average = Sum/ count
PRINT Sum, Average
```

Turbo Pascal Solution

```
Program Cal;

Uses Crt;
Var
        Count: Integer;
        X, Sum: Integer;
        Average: real;
Begin
   For Count := 1 to 10 DO     {This will repeat ten times}
   Begin
        Read(X); {this statement will be executed 10 times}
        Sum:= Sum + X; {calculation of sum}
   End;
   Average:=Sum/count; {calculation of Average}
   Write(Sum); {Prints the sum on the user's screen}
   Write(Average); {prints the average on the user's screen}
End.
```

C Solution

```
# include <conio.h>

int count, X, Sum;
float Average;

void main()
{
        For(count= 1; count<=10; count++)
        {
                scanf("%d",&X);
                Sum=Sum+X;
        }
        Average = Sum/count;
        printf("%d",&Sum);
        printf("%f",&Average);
}
```

Activity 1

Write a program to read the number of students in a class in the variable amount. For each student, your program should read their grade and name.

Activity 2
Write a program to print your three times timetable on the screen, for number ranging from one (1) to twenty.

Sample output:
```
        3 X 1 = 3
        3 X 2 = 6
        ............
        ............
        3 X 20 = 60
```

REPEAT UNTIL Loop

A very simple and easy to use a post-test loop in Pascal is the Repeat....Until loop. This loop repeats a set of statements, for an undetermined number of times until a condition becomes true.

Repeat
>   Statement 1
>   Statement 2
>   ....

Until (condition)

Example 1 Write a program to get a set of numbers from the user until a negative number is entered.
Negative numbers and less than zero

Solution

```
Program numchecker;
Uses crt;
Var
        Num: Integer; {this will hold the value entered}
Begin
   Repeat
        Write('Please enter a number');{prompts for a number}
        Read(Num);{allows the user to input a number}
   Until(Num < 0);
End.
```

The program will prompt for a number repeatedly until a number lesser than zero (a negative number) is entered.

Example 2: Write a program to read a set of students' name and grade, the program should terminate when a student by the name "Kamala" with grade =99 is entered. At the end of the program, print the number of students that were entered.

SOLUTION
Program StudCount;

Uses crt;
Var
        Name: String;
        Grade: Real;
        Count: Integer;   (The loop starts here.)
Begin
        Repeat
            Count: = Count + 1;
            Read(name);   {Body of the Loop}
            Read(grade);
        Until(name= "Kamala") AND (grade = 99);
        Write(Count);
End.

(The testing is done at a the end of the loop (Post-test))

Activity 1
Write a program to get a set of grades from the user, until the grade -1 is entered. The number of grades entered should be printed at the end of the program.

Activity 2
A program is needed that will accept two numbers from the user, and a character. If the character is 's', your program should calculate and print the sum of the two numbers, if the character is 'p', it should calculate and print the product of the two numbers. The program should terminate when the character entered is 'x'.

Array

An array is an ordered set of components that are of the same type. By using a suitable selector, individual components may be accessed and modified. Arrays are simple to use and implement.

You may think of an array as a list of grades or cars or fruits. In other words, you cannot have both Integers and string in the same array; only one type is permissible.

Each item/ element in the array has a unique index. The first element in the array is indexed one (1), the second one is index one (2) and so on.

Array: Jam4

Index	1	2	3	4
Elements	Michael Frater,	Nesta Carter	Usain Bolt	Asafa Powell

The array above has four elements, which are indexed from 1 to 4. To access Usain Bolt, you would write the array name with the corresponding index in open and closed square brackets. i.e.

Jam4 [1] ←   **"Michael Frater"**
Jam4 [2] ←   **"Nesta Carter"**
Jam4 [3] ←   **"Usain Bolt"**
Jam5 [4] ←   **"Asafa Powell"**

Assigning Values to an array

To assign a value to an array, write the array name and index, then the assignment statement (=) followed by the value to be assigned to the array:

Example

Write an algorithm to assign the even numbers between 1 and 10 to an array **Even**.

Even [1] = 2
Even [2] = 4
Even [3] = 6
Even [4] = 8

*This could also be done using a loop:
Index = 1
For Count = 1 to 9 DO
        IF (Count mod 2 = 0) THEN
            Even [Index] = Count
            Index=Index + 1
      End If
ENDFOR

Mod returns the remainder when a number is divided by another number. When even numbers are divided by 2 their remainder is 0.

* Draw a table to show what the content of Even would look like now!!!

Reading Data From the Keyboard into an Array

Elements are inputted into an array, using an INPUT statement, followed by the array's name and the index to which the element is to be stored in. This process can be achieved by writing an INPUT statement for each element or by using a loop. E.g. write a program to get the scores of ten students from the user, in an Array **Grade**.

Solution	Or Using a Loop
INPUT Grade[1]	FOR Count = 1 to 10 Do
INPUT Grade[2]	INPUT Grade[Count]
INPUT Grade[3]	ENDFOR
INPUT Grade[4]	
INPUT Grade[5]	
INPUT Grade[6]	
INPUT Grade[7]	
INPUT Grade[8]	
INPUT Grade[9]	
INPUT Grade[10]	

You may view Grade as:

Index/Count	1	2	3	4	5	6	7	8	9	10
Grade										

Each time in the loop, the value that the user entered will be written in the appropriate index, as the value of count changes from zero (0) upwards. * As count changes, the index pointer moves.

Consider the following Inputs for grades: 60, 70, 80, 76, 19, 98, 67, 98, 100, 56

59

In the array the values would appear as follows:

Index/Count	Grade
1	60
2	70
3	80
4	76
5	19
6	98
7	67
8	98
9	100
10	56

Therefore: Grade [1] = 60, Grade [6] = 98 and so on.

Printing the Content of an Array

Just like the Input, the content of the array can be printed by writing the array's name and the different index, or by using a loop.

Example: Write a program to print the content of the Array Grade

Solution	Or Using a Loop
PRINT Grade[1]	FOR Count = 1 to 10 Do
PRINT Grade[2]	PRINT Grade[Count]
PRINT Grade[3]	ENDFOR
PRINT Grade[4]	
PRINT Grade[5]	
PRINT Grade[6]	
PRINT Grade[7]	
PRINT Grade[8]	
PRINT Grade[9]	
PRINT Grade[10]	

* **Which of the methods would you use to print the content of an array?**

Activity 1

Write an algorithm to get the amount of money paid by ten students in an array **Fee.** Print the total amount of money paid at the end of the program.

Activity 2

Write an algorithm to print the content of the array **Fee**.

Linear Search

Searches are normally carried out to check if an element or elements are present in an array. A linear search is a sequential search that is carried out on each element in an array to check if it matches a certain Item. Consider the following algorithm, in which the index of element 120, is being searched for.

Example: Consider the following array **Weight:**

Index	1	2	3	4	5
Element	10	20	50	120	60

Write an algorithm to traverse the array **Weight** and print the index where the weight 120 is located.

Solution

FOR count = 1 to 5 DO *{this will loop from 1 to the end of the array (5) or}*
Begin   *{until the value if found}*
        If(Weight[count] = 120) DO *{Checks if the array element is 120}*
                Print count *{the index(count) is printed if the element is 120}*
                Halt/ stop searching *{Halt forces the program to stop}*
        End IF
ENDFOR

Solution II

Found = false
Arraysize =5
count = 1   *{1 is the array's first index}*
WHILE (count <= Arraysize AND found = false)DO
        If(Weight[count] = 120) DO
                Print count
                found = True
        EndIf
        count=count + 1 *{this increments/ increases count by one}*
ENDWHILE
        IF(found = false)THEN
                PRINT "Weight not found" *{This is printed if item not found}*
        ENDIF

the loop will stop when found= true **or** count is bigger than 5

Found is assigned the value true, since Weight[count]=120

61

Array in Pascal

Just like your variables, an array has to be declared before it can be used by the computer. An array is declared as follows:

> Arrayname : Array [index type] of <Element Type>;

The element type can be of any Type, but the index type must be Integer

Example: Declare an array **Grades** that will store integer grades for ten students:

> **SOLUTION**
>
> Grades: Array[1..10] of Integer;

Example 2: Declare an array name that will store the names of the thirty different items sold in a store.

> **SOLUTION**
>
> Name: Array[0..29] of String;

Example 3 Declare an array Pay that will store the pay of the 100 members that work in a factory.

> **SOLUTION**
> Pay: Array[1..100] of real;

Basic Array Input in Pascal

Example 1

Write a program to read five integers from the user in the array Choice;

SOLUTION

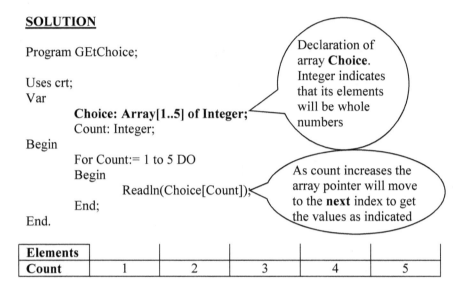

Program GEtChoice;

Uses crt;
Var
    Choice: Array[1..5] of Integer;
    Count: Integer;
Begin
    For Count:= 1 to 5 DO
    Begin
        Readln(Choice[Count]);
    End;
End.

Declaration of array **Choice**. Integer indicates that its elements will be whole numbers

As count increases the array pointer will move to the **next** index to get the values as indicated

Elements					
Count	1	2	3	4	5

Example 2
Write a program to get the scores of ten students from the user, in an Array **Grade**.

Program getGrades;

Uses crt;
Var
    Grade: Array[1..10] of integer;
    Count:Integer;
Begin
    For Count:= 1 to 10 DO
    Begin
        Readln(Grade[Count]);
    End;
End.

Improve on the algorithm in Example 2, to compute and print the average grade.

Basic Array Output in Pascal

Example 3

Write a program to print the content of the array Grade;


```pascal
Program DisplayGrades;

Uses crt;
Var
        Grade: Array[1..10] of integer;
        Count:Integer;
Begin
        For Count:= 1 to 10 DO
        Begin
                Writeln(Grade[Count]);
        End;
End.
```

* Study the codes and discuss the changes made with your friends and teacher.

Linear Search in Pascal

```pascal
Program LinearSearch;
Uses Crt;
Const
        Arraysize=5; {the array size will remain unchanged}
Var
        Found: Boolean; {This can be true or false}
        Count:Integer;
        Weight: Array[1..Arraysize] of integer;{*Arraysize = 5}
Begin
        Found := false;
        Count := 1;
        WHILE (count <= Arraysize) AND (found = false)DO
        Begin
          If(Weight[count] = 120) DO
          Begin
                Writeln(count);
                found := True;
          End;
          Count:=Count + 1; {this increments/ increases count by one}
        End;
END.
```

64

Testing

Before a program is released to its users, it must be carefully tested for errors/ bugs. Testing involves a series of activities that ensure that a program works correctly and produces the correct result. Below is a description of some of the activities that are carried out during testing:

Debugging

Debugging is the detection, location, and correction of faults (bugs) causing errors in a program. The errors are detected by observing **error messages** or by finding unexpected results in the test output. Debugging is normally done by a program known as a debugger.

Dry run

This is a manual walkthrough of a section of a program. This is useful for locating errors, particularly runtime errors.

Debugging is normally done by a program (debugger) however dry-run is a manual check.

Logical Error

Logical errors are mistakes in the design of the program, such as a branch to a wrong statement or the use of an inappropriate mathematical formula. *A logical error will be recognized because the program produces wrong results or an incorrect display.*

Syntax Error

Syntax errors result from the violation of the rules governing a programming language. Example: spelling a keyword such as Write (in Pascal) incorrectly.

Runtime Error

These are flaws detected during the program execution. A popular runtime error is a division by zero; this may occur where the user supplies zero as the denominator for a fraction, and so on.

Test Data
This refers to sample data entered into a program to test its functionality.

Source Code

This is a program written in a programming language.

Object code

This is a machine language program produced by a compiler.

Compiling

This is the process of converting source code to object code. Compiling is done by a program known as a compiler.

Sentinel Value- a special value used to terminate a loop

Assembler
An assembler is a program that converts assembly language codes to machine codes.

Executing the program
Execute (a program)
The process of transferring program instructions from a storage medium into memory.

- Program loading – copying a program from hard disk to the main memory in order to put the program in a ready-to-run state.
- Linking – combining various pieces of code and data together to form a single executable object code that can be loaded into memory.

Variable A name that represents a piece of data that can take many possible values

Strcmp – A C/ C++ function that compare character strings. The equal sign (=) cannot be used for string comparison in **C**. E.g. in your algorithm you may have IF(name="Kat"); but in C/C++ it would be if(!strcmp(name, "Kat"))

Basic Signs and Symbols

Description	QBasic	Pascal	C/ C++
=	Equality and Assignment	Equality	Assignment
= =	N/A	N/A	Equality
:=	N/A	Assignment	N/A
<>	Not Equal	Not Equal	N/A
!=	N/A	N/A	Not Equal
%	N/A	N/A	Modulation
$	String	N/A	N/A
++	N/A	N/A	Increment
--	N/A	N/A	Decrement
&	N/A	N/A	Address
!	N/A	N/A	Logical Negation

VIEW YOUR ANSWERS BY SECTION

UNIT II - *Problem Partitioning*

i.	Processing
ii.	Input
iii.	Processing
iv.	Storage
v.	Output

Correct order: iii, ii, v, i, iv

Using Input And Assignment Statements

Activity 2

INPUT Joy
INPUT Peace
Love ← Joy * Peace

Activity 3

INPUT Cat, Rat, Bat
Sum ← Cat + Rat + Bat
Average ← Sum / 3

*It is ok if you used different variables from Cat, Rat, Bat

Activity 4

1	GCT_Rate ← 0.165	Initialization of the GCT rate to 0.165
2	INPUT Price	Get a Price from the user.
3	GCT ← Price * GCT_Rate	Calculation of GCT amount
4	Total ← Price + GCT	Calculation of Total cost after GCT

Activity 2

PRINT "Please enter the first value"
INPUT Joy
PRINT "Please enter the second value"
INPUT Peace
    Love ← Joy * Peace
PRINT Love

Activity 3

Please "Enter the first number"
INPUT Cat
PRINT "Please enter the second number"
INPUT Rat
PRINT "Please enter the third number"
INPUT Bat
    Sum ← Cat + Rat + Bat
    Average ← Sum / 3
PRINT "The Average is", Average

Activity 4

Study the following algorithm and explain what it does:

1	GCT_Rate ← 0.165	Initialize GCT rate to .165
2	PRINT "Please enter the Price"	Prompt for the price
3	INPUT Price	Get the price from the user
4	GCT ← Price * GCT_Rate	Compute GCT
5	Total ← Price + GCT	Compute overall cost
6	PRINT GCT	Display GCT amount
	PRINT "The total cost is", Total	Display a message followed by the Total **Cost**

Task 1

PRINT "Please the Hour of Arrival"
INPUT Hour
PRNT "Please enter the Minute of Arrival"
INPUT Minute
IF (Hour > 5) THEN
  Hminutes ← (Hour-5) / 60
  TotalMin ← Hminutes + Minute
  Cost ← TotalMin * 10
  PRINT Cost
ELSE
  PRINT "No Late fee required"
ENDIF

Task 2

INPUT num
IF num < 0 THEN
  Square ← num * num
ELSE
  Cube ← num * num * num
ENDIF
PRINT Square
PRINT Cube

WHILE

Activity 1

Final ← 0
Total_cost ← 0
INPUT name
INPUT quantity
INPUT price
WHILE name <> "end" DO
      Total_cost ← quantity * price
      Final ← Final + Total_cost
      INPUT name
      INPUT quantity
      INPUT price
END WHILE

Activity 2

ACount ← 0
BCount ← 0
INPUT name, class
WHILE name <> "Freda" DO
      IF class = "7a" THEN
            ACount ← ACount + 1
      ENDIF
      IF class = "7b" THEN
            BCount ← BCount +1
      END
      INPUT name, class
ENDWHILE
PRINT ACount, BCount

Activity 1

```
FOR count = 1 to 11 DO
      INPUT size
ENDFOR
```

Activity 2

```
FOR count = 1 to 10 DO
      INPUT num
      Sum ← Sum + num
ENDFOR
Average ← Sum / count
PRINT Sum, Average
```

Activity 3

```
READ amount
FOR count = 1 to amount DO
      READ name, gender
ENDFOR
```

Activity 4
```
maleCount ← 0
femaleCount ← 0
READ amount
FOR count = 1 to amount DO
      READ name, gender
      IF gender = male THEN
            maleCount ← maleCount + 1
      ELSE
            femaleCount ← femaleCount + 1
      ENDIF
ENDFOR
PRINT maleCount, femaleCount
```

TRACE TABLE

Task 1

Count	num	SMALLEST	LARGEST
1	100	100	100
2	30	**30**	100
3	200	30	**200**

Task 2

Product
2
4
8
16

Task 3

COUNT	X	PRINT
1	2	-
1	4	1, 4
6	6	6,6
11	8	11, 8
16	10	16, 10
21	12	21, 12
26		

CONDITIONAL STATEMENTS

Activity 1

QUICK BASIC Solution

```
INPUT gender$
IF gender$ = "Female" THEN
        PRINT "Room9"
ENDIF
IF gender$ = "Male" THEN
        PRINT "Room1"
ENDIF
```

TURBO PASCAL Solution

```
Program rooms;
Uses crt;
Var
        Gender: string;

Begin
        Read(Gender);
        If(gender = "Female")THEN
                Write("Room9");
        IF(gender = "Male")THEN
                Write("Room1");
End.
```

C Solution

```c
# include<conio.h>

char gender[10];
void main()
{
        scanf("%s",&gender);
        if(!strcmp(gender, "male"))
                printf("Room 9");
        if(!strcmp(gender,"female"))
                printf("Room 1");
}
```

WHILE LOOP

Activity 1

Quick Basic Solution

```
X = 5
K = 5
SUM = 5
WHILE  SUM < 75
        SUM = SUM + K
        PRINT K
        K = K + X
WEND
PRINT SUM
```

Turbo Pascal Solution

```pascal
Program mything;

Uses crt;
Var
        X, Y, SUM, K: Integer;
Begin
        While (Sum <75) do
        Begin
                SUM:=SUM + K;
                Write(K);
                K:=K+X;
        End;
        Write(SUM);
End.
```

C Solution

```c
# include<conio.h>

int X, Y, SUM, K;

void main()
{
        while(SUM < 75)
        {
                SUM = SUM + K;
                printf("%d",K);
                K = K + X;
        }
        printf("%d",SUM);
}
```

Activity 2

QUICK BASIC Solution

```
Count = 0
INPUT grade
WHILE (grade <> -1)
        Count = Count + 1
        INPUT grade
WEND
PRINT Count
```

TURBO PASCAL Solution

```
Program Mystyle;
Uses crt;

Var
        Count, grade: Integer;
Begin
        Count := 0
        Read(grade);
        WHILE (grade <> -1)DO
        Begin
                Count := Count + 1;
                Read(grade);
        End;
        Write(Count);
End.
```

C Solution

```c
# include<conio.h>

int Count, grade;

void main()
{
        Count = 0;
        scanf("%d",&grade);
        while(grade != -1          )
        {
                Count=Count+1;
                scanf("%d",&grade);
        }
        printf("%d",Count);
}
```

FOR LOOP

Activity 1

QUICK BASIC Solution

```
INPUT amount

FOR Count = 1 to amount DO
        INPUT grade
        INPUT name$
NEXT
```

TURBO PASCAL Solution

Program forloop;

Uses crt;

Var
        Count, amount, grade: Integer;
        name: String;
Begin
        For Count: = 1 to amount Do
        Begin
                Read(grade);
                Read(name);
        End;
End.

C Solution

```
# include<conio.h>

int Count, amount, grade;
char name[20];

void main()
{
        for(Count = 1; Count<=amount; Count ++)
        {
                scanf("%d",&grade);
                scanf("%c",&name);
        }
}
```

Activity 2

TURBO PASCAL SOLUTION

```
Program TimeTable;
Uses crt;
Var
        Count: Integer;
Begin
        For Count:=1 to 20 DO {this will loop from 1 to 20}
                Write('3 X ',Count,'=',3*Count);
End.
```

The value of Count is multiplied by 3 each time to get and print the answer

*The portion of the Write statement that is enclosed in the quotation will be printed as a text in its original form. However the value of Count, and 3 * Count will be printed since they are not enclosed in quotations.*

e.g if count = 6. the output would be:
3 X 6 = 18

REPEAT UNTIL LOOP

Activity 1

```
Program GetGrades;
Uses crt;
Var
        GCount, grade: Integer; {variable declaration}

Begin
        GCount:=0;
        Repeat
                Write('Enter a grade');
                Read(grade);

                GCount:= GCount + 1;
        Until (grade = -1);
        Write('The total number of grades entered is',GCount);
End.
```

Activity 2

```
Program calculator;
Uses crt;
Var
        num1, num2: Integer;
        ch: char;
Begin
   Repeat
        Write('Enter the first number');
        Read (num1);
        Write('Enter the second number');
        Read(num2);
        Writeln('Select a choice:');
        Write('[s]...Sum      [P]....Product');
        Read(ch);
        If(ch='s')Then
        Begin
                Sum:=num1 + num2;
                Write('The sum is:',Sum);
        End;
        If(ch='p')Then
        Begin
                Product:=num1 * num2;
                Write('The Product is:',Product);
        End;
   Until(Ch='x');
End.
```

UNIT VII - Array

ARRAY

Activity 1

Write an algorithm to get the amount of money paid by ten students in an array **Fee**. Print the total amount of money paid at the end of the program.

SOLUTION
```
FOR count = 1 to 10 DO
        INPUT Fee[count]
        Total = Total + Fee[count]
ENDFOR
Print "The amount of money paid is", Total
```

Activity 2

Write an algorithm to print the content of the array **Fee**.
SOLUTION
```
FOR count = 1 to 10 DO
        PRINT Fee[count]
ENDFOR
```

Example 2 Improved

Example 2
Write a program to get the scores of ten students from the user, in an Array **Grade**.

```
Program getGrades;
Uses crt;
Var
        Grade: Array[1..10] of integer; {declaration of array}
        Count:Integer; {this variable holds the amount of grades}
        Sum:Integer; {this variable will hold the total of the grades}
        Average:Real; {this holds the average grade}
Begin
        For Count:= 1 to 10 DO
        Begin
                Readln(Grade[Count]);
                Sum:= Sum + Grade[Count]);
        End;
        Average:=Sum/Count; {Calculation of Average}
        Writeln('The average is',Average); {Displays the average}
End.
```

83

References

Brian D. Hahn, R. K. (2001). *Pascal for Students.* Oxford: Newnes.

Deitel, H. D. (2001). *C++ How TO Program.* New Jersey: Prentice Hall.

Gilberg, B. A. (2007). *Computer Science, A Structured Programming Approach Using C.* Boston, United States of America: GEX Publishing Services.

Kalelioglu, F. (2015). A new way of teaching programming skills to K-12 students. *Computers in Human Behavior, 52*, 200-210.

Koh, S. Y. (2014). Review on teaching and learning of computational thinking through programming: What is next for K-12? *Computers in Human Behavior, 41*, 51-61.

Lee, I. A. (2017). Preparing STEM Teachers to offer New Mexico Computer Science for All. *2017 ACM SIGCSE Technical Symposium on Computer Science Education,* 363-368.

Shammas, N. C. (1993). *Teach Yourself QBasic in 21 Days.* USA: Prentice Hall.

www.ingramcontent.com/pod-product-compliance
Lightning Source LLC
Chambersburg PA
CBHW070851070326
40690CB00009B/1789